NEW VANGUARD • 147

AMERICAN LIGHT AND MEDIUM FRIGATES 1794–1836

MARK LARDAS

ILLUSTRATED BY TONY BRYAN
& GIUSEPPE RAVA

First published in Great Britain in 2008 by Osprey Publishing,
Midland House, West Way, Botley, Oxford, OX2 0PH, UK
443 Park Avenue South, New York, NY 10016, USA
E-mail: info@ospreypublishing.com

© 2008 Osprey Publishing Ltd.

All rights reserved. Apart from any fair dealing for the purpose of private study, research, criticism or review, as permitted under the Copyright, Designs and Patents Act, 1988, no part of this publication may be reproduced, stored in a retrieval system, or transmitted in any form or by any means, electronic, electrical, chemical, mechanical, optical, photocopying, recording or otherwise, without the prior written permission of the copyright owner. Inquiries should be addressed to the Publishers.

A CIP catalog record for this book is available from the British Library

ISBN: 978 1 84603 266 0

Page layout by Melissa Orrom Swan, Oxford
Index by Glyn Sutcliffe
Typeset in Sabon and Myriad Pro
Originated by PPS Grasmere Ltd, Leeds
Printed in China through Worldprint

08 09 10 11 12   10 9 8 7 6 5 4 3 2 1

FOR A CATALOG OF ALL BOOKS PUBLISHED BY OSPREY MILITARY AND AVIATION PLEASE CONTACT:

NORTH AMERICA
Osprey Direct, c/o Random House Distribution Center, 400 Hahn Road, Westminster, MD 21157
E-mail: info@ospreydirect.com

ALL OTHER REGIONS
Osprey Direct UK, P.O. Box 140 Wellingborough, Northants, NN8 2FA, UK
E-mail: info@ospreydirect.co.uk

Osprey Publishing is supporting the Woodland Trust, the UK's leading woodland conservation charity, by funding the dedication of trees.

www.ospreypublishing.com

AUTHOR'S NOTE

The following abbreviations indicate the sources of the illustrations used in this volume:

AC – Author's Collection
FDRL – Franklin Delano Roosevelt Presidential Library Collection
LOC – Library of Congress
USNA-R – United States Naval Academy Robinson Print Collection
USNHF – US Navy Historical Foundation
Other sources are listed in full.

AUTHOR'S DEDICATION

This book is dedicated to my friends in the Gulf Coast Historic Ship Modelers Association. Gentlepeople, scholars, and modelers all.

EDITOR'S NOTE

For ease of comparison between types, imperial measurements are used almost exclusively throughout this book. The following data will help in converting the imperial measurements to metric:

1 mile = 1.6km
1lb = 0.45kg
1 yard = 0.9m
1ft = 0.3m
1in. = 2.54cm/25.4mm
1 gal = 4.5 liters
1 ton (US) = 0.9 tonnes

CONTENTS

INTRODUCTION   4

DESIGN AND DEVELOPMENT   6
- The frigate
- Prior American experience and foreign trends
- The Federal Navy
- The American frigate reconsidered
- The War of 1812 and after

OPERATIONAL HISTORY   16
- The Quasi-War
- The Barbary Wars
- The War of 1812
- 1815 and afterwards

THE SHIPS   30
- Frigates rated 44 guns
- Frigates rated 36 guns
- Frigates rated 32 guns
- Prize frigates

GLOSSARY   44

BIBLIOGRAPHY   47

INDEX   48

AMERICAN LIGHT AND MEDIUM FRIGATES 1794–1836

INTRODUCTION

The American frigate made a brave sight as it sailed from Boston harbor on a bright June morning in 1813. The ship was already as obsolete as a tricorne hat, but the hopeful crowds that watched either did not know it or did not care. Fourteen years earlier a slightly smaller American frigate had triumphed over a French frigate even larger than the British ship waiting outside the harbor. Moreover, only the previous year the Americans had thumped the Royal Navy in three successive frigate duels. Few thought this battle would be any different.

The British frigate was equally obsolete, and three near-sisters had fallen before the guns of the large American 44-gun frigates. The Royal Navy was withdrawing this class of frigate from North American waters and replacing them with larger ships as quickly as they became available. This particular British frigate was overdue for relief. Its captain, aware that an American frigate was ready to sail, had lingered outside the American port, hoping to lure it into battle. That morning he had sent in a challenge to his Yankee counterpart. The captain of this British frigate, the *Shannon*, had several advantages over unluckier peers on the near-sisters *Guerriere*, *Macedonian*, and *Java*. While his opponent, the USS *Chesapeake*, was originally rated at 44 guns, it was designed to carry a broadside of 18lb cannon, not the 24lb guns of the other American 44-gun frigates. (For more about the system of ratings, see "The Ships" chapter below.) Where the other British frigates had to face a broadside 50 percent larger than the ones they carried, the broadsides of the *Chesapeake* and *Shannon* were virtually identical.

The crew of the *Shannon* had been together for nearly seven years. The *Chesapeake* was just starting its commission, with a new and inexperienced crew. Furthermore, the *Shannon*'s captain was a gunnery fanatic – he drilled his crew daily, and frequently conducted live fire drills, aiming at marks.

The battle, when joined, lasted 15 minutes, and was one of the bloodiest quarter-hours in naval history, with heavy casualties on both sides. Experience told: at the end of the battle, the white ensign flew over the Stars and Stripes, but at a high cost. The American captain was dead, and the British captain so badly wounded that he never went to sea again. Both ships were so critically damaged that neither saw further active service.

The lion triumphed over the upstart eagle because of an error made 13 years earlier. The nascent US Navy had fundamentally misinterpreted its first naval victory, and had abandoned construction of the pre-1800 type of frigate

OPPOSITE
Boston fought and captured the French corvette *Berceau* after a furious battle on October 12, 1801. The battle matched *Boston*'s 12lb guns against *Berceau*'s 9-pdrs. (USNHF)

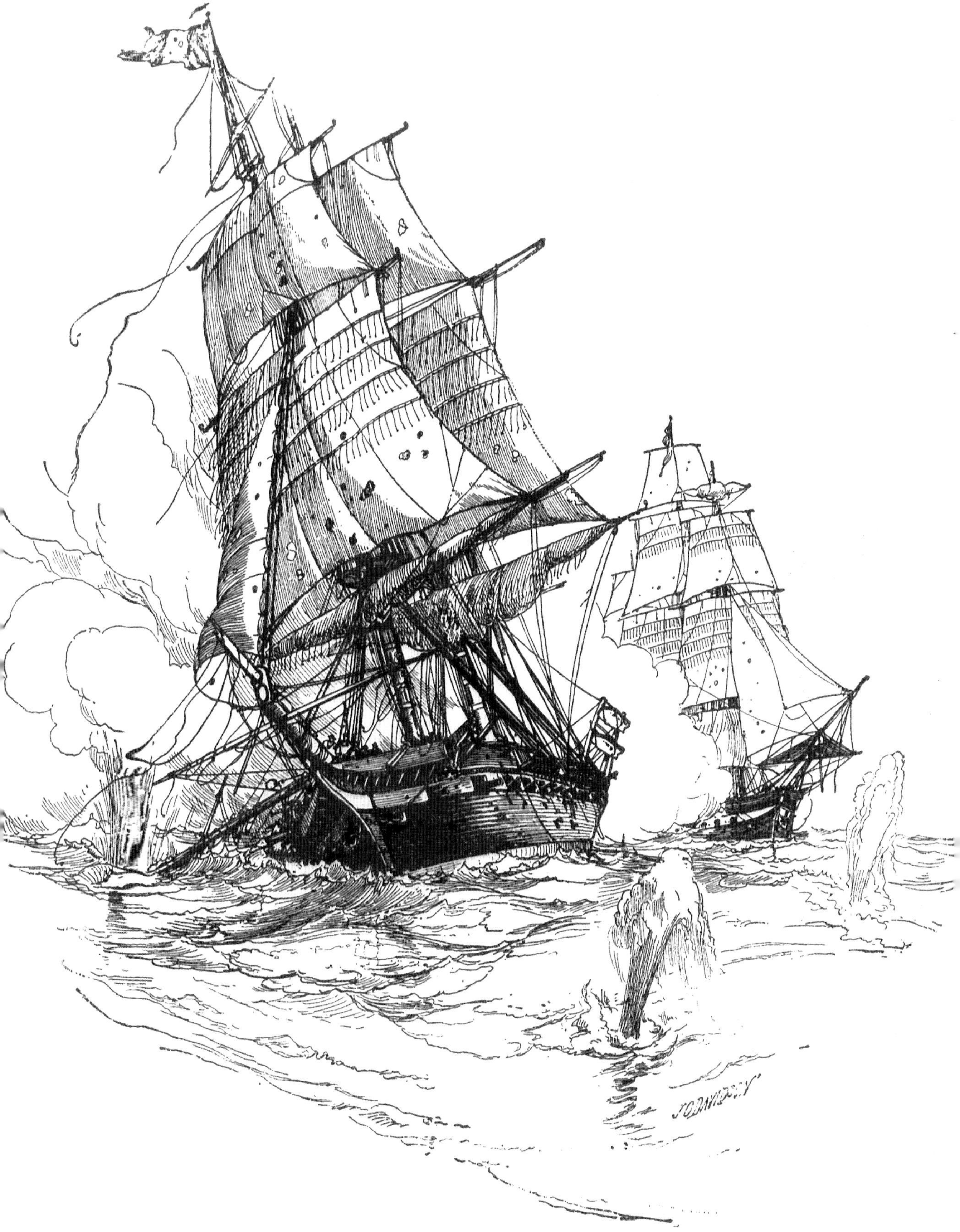

The frigate *Chesapeake* sails out of Boston harbor at noon on June 1, 1813, to fight HMS *Shannon*. (FDRL)

Truxton was one of the first six captains appointed to the US Navy in 1794, and assigned to oversee the construction of the *Constellation*, in Baltimore. In 1794, with Fox's assistance, Truxton wrote a book entitled *A System of Masting*. It advocated building smaller, handier frigates.

Truxton commanded the *Constellation* during the Quasi-War with France, defeating two large French frigates with his 36-gun vessel. The US Navy's two 44-gun frigates in commission during 1798 were less lucky. They failed to catch any French frigates, and proved slow sailing ships, which matched the European navies' experiences with large frigates, especially those armed with a main battery of 24lb guns. The French 24lb frigates were routinely being captured by British 38-gun frigates. British experiments with 24lb frigates were equally mixed. Only the *Indefatigable*, a 44-gun frigate razeed from a 64-gun ship-of-the-line, had a notable career. What success the others had could equally have been achieved by a standard 38-gun frigate armed with 18lb guns.

Unfortunately, the wrong lesson was taken from the *Constellation*'s victories. Ignored was a major cause for the *Constellation*'s swift success against the *Insurgente*, which it captured in 1799 after a gun battle (see below). *Constellation* carried a battery of 28 24lb guns in that battle, not the intended 18lb guns.

A USS *BOSTON* SAIL PLAN

Boston is here shown as it appeared during the Barbary Wars, in 1802. White had not yet replaced buff as the US Navy's detail color of choice by then, and a wide gun port strake was still used.

Another difference by 1801 was the sail plan. The masts and spars were significantly larger than the original versions. The royal sails, which would have been rigged flying, on the top of the topgallant masts in 1799, were now set on separate royal masts, above the topgallant masts.

Initially armed exclusively with long guns – 24 12-pdrs on the gun deck and eight 9-pdrs on the quarterdeck and forecastle – *Boston* was rearmed before sailing to the Mediterranean. It carried 26 12lb long guns on the gun deck, six 9lb long guns and 12 32lb carronades on the upper works, 48 guns in all. This battery may explain why *Boston* never saw active service after its 1802 cruise ended. The ship was designed to carry 24 12lb and eight 6lb long guns, a total weight of 91,000lb. Its Barbary War battery weighed one-third more: 122,000lb. Since the heaviest guns were carried at the ends, *Boston* would have been subject to severe hogging strains, which would have weakened the hull significantly.

A USS *BOSTON* SAIL PLAN

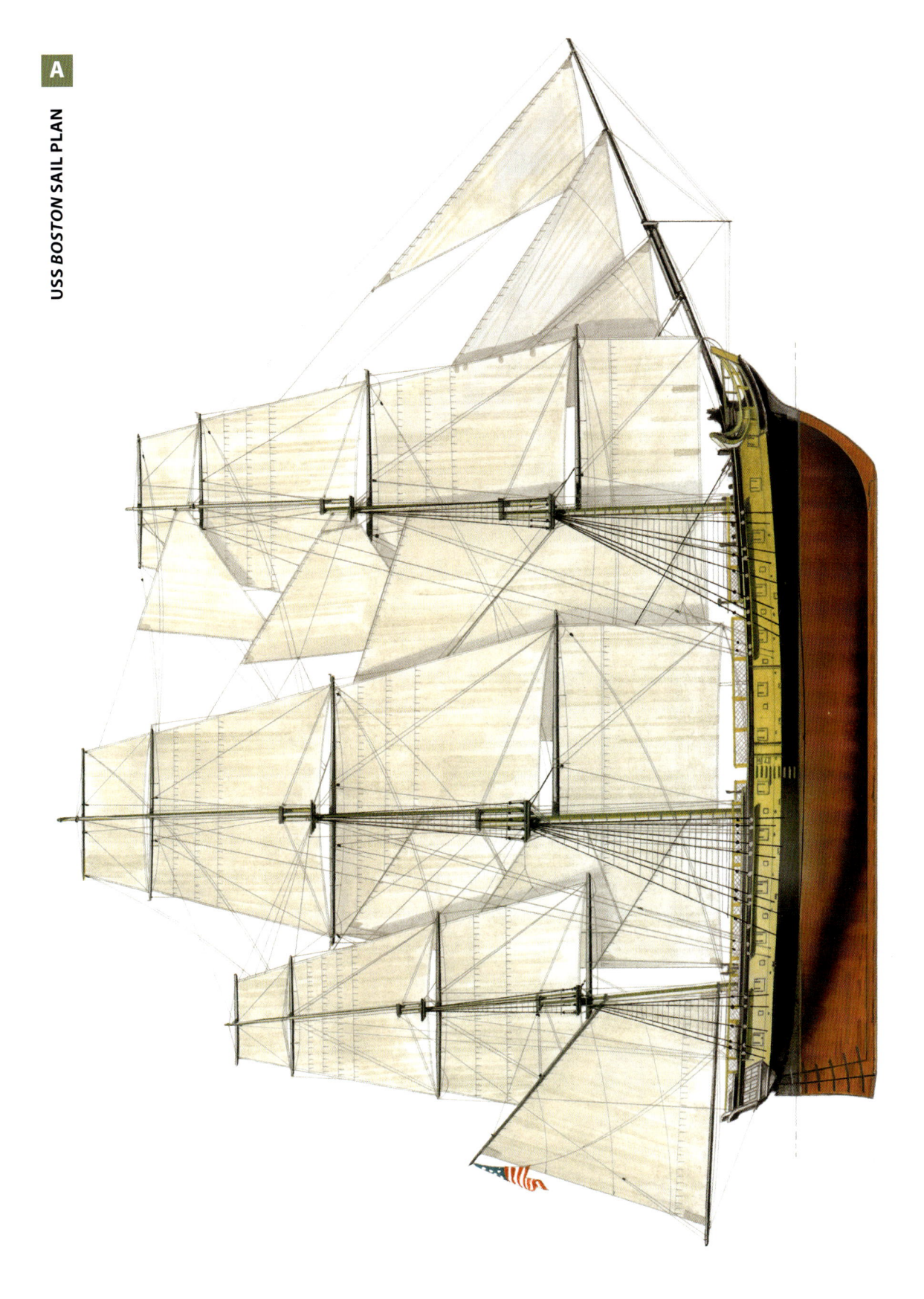

The result of campaigning by Fox, foreign disappointment with the 24lb frigate, and the experience of the first year of the Quasi-War led to a reassessment of American frigate design, with smaller frigates becoming the order of the day. The Navy let Fox redesign the sixth frigate authorized in 1794. It remained a 44-gun frigate, scaled on European dimensions. The ship, named *Chesapeake*, was much smaller than Humphreys' 44s – at 152ft 6in. long with a beam of 40ft, it was even shorter and shallower than Humphreys' 36-gun frigates. It was also designed to carry a main battery of 28 18lb guns, with 16 9lb guns on the upper works. The ship reemphasized the quarterdeck and forecastle. As designed, the spar deck over the waist was lighter than those on the Humphreys frigates.

The Josiah Fox-designed *Philadelphia* under construction in Joshua Humphreys' shipyard. *Philadelphia* is identified as a 44-gun frigate in this period drawing and was rated as such for its entire career. (USNHF)

Fox followed this up by designing the largest of the subscription frigates, *Philadelphia*. It too was rated at 44 guns. At 157ft long and with a beam of 39ft, it displaced less tonnage than the *Chesapeake*, and was also intended to carry a battery of 18lb guns on the gun deck. Ironically, *Philadelphia* was built in Joshua Humphreys' yard.

Despite many after-the-fact claims, *Chesapeake* and *Philadelphia* were intended as 44-gun frigates, and were carried by the US Navy as 44-gun frigates on the Navy's list through 1807. *Chesapeake* was the flagship of the Mediterranean Squadron in 1802–03, and was again sailing to the Mediterranean in 1807 at the time of the *Chesapeake–Leopard* Affair (described in detail later) as squadron flagship (this was a task assigned to 44-gun frigates).

By European standards, at the end of the 1790s those frigates were 44-gun frigates. They were larger than the British 38-gun frigates, and roughly the same size as French 40-gun and 44-gun frigates. *Chesapeake*, laid up in ordinary after 1807, reappeared on the Navy list as a 36-gun frigate in 1812. Other frigates were then being re-rated, some as the result of rebuilds.

The other frigates built during this period showed similar downsizing. Three of the four remaining subscription frigates, and both *Adams* and *General Green* (contracted by the Navy), were rated at 32 guns. While all five were carried on the Navy's lists as 32-gun frigates, three – *John Adams*, *Adams*, and *General Greene* – were smaller than the other two, *Essex* and *Boston*. They are frequently referred to as "28-gun frigates."

All five were anomalous ships. The rest of the worlds' navies were abandoning the 12lb frigate in the late 1790s, but these vessels took 12lb guns as their primary armament. While a match for European light frigates and superior to these navies' ship-sloops and corvettes, the American 12lb frigates would be overwhelmed by the firepower of both French and British standard frigates, with 18lb batteries. This situation worsened in the next decade as the older 12lb frigates of foreign navies were replaced by new construction with 18lb batteries. These ships still had some use, and provided valuable service over the next few years. Indeed, they were outstanding designs, with the *Essex* designed by William Hackett, who earlier designed the *Alliance*. Regardless, they were obsolescent when their keels touched saltwater.

Other than the *Philadelphia*, the 36-gun *New York* was the only subscription frigate capable of carrying an 18lb battery. It was designed by Samuel Humphreys, Joshua Humphreys' son. But this vessel was 20ft shorter than his father's 36-gun frigates. The US Navy also captured seven frigate-sized vessels between 1798 and 1815. Three were incorporated into the Navy: the French *Insurgente*, and the Royal Navy's *Macedonian* and *Cyane*. *Insurgente* was a French 36-gun frigate, a class normally armed with 26 12lb and ten 6lb guns. When captured it carried four carronades, and was described as a "40-gun frigate." It was taken into the US Navy as *Insurgent*. The *Macedonian* was a British 38-gun standard frigate, designed to carry 18lb guns on the gun deck. The *Cyane* was rated as a post ship in the Royal Navy, rather than a frigate. It carried guns on its quarterdeck and forecastle, so the Americans claimed it as a frigate when it was captured.

USS *Macedonian* under sail off Boston in 1822. While the frigate remained a prestigious prize after the War of 1812, to the point where the Navy replaced it with a near replica, its influence on American warship design was negligible. (FDRL)

The prize ships had little influence on American ship design, although both *Macedonian* and *Cyane* were used for many years as American warships.

The War of 1812 and after

The frigates built for the Quasi-War were completed by 1801. They were the last frigates built for the US Navy until the War of 1812. By then, the shortcomings of the American 12lb and even 18lb frigates were clear. Most of the survivors were converted to ship-sloops by cutting down the quarterdeck and forecastle. The process started in the War of 1812, when the *Adams* was so converted, and it was joined after the war by the *John Adams* and the prize vessel *Cyane*.

As the hulls of the surviving light and standard frigates wore out, they were replaced by new ships with the same name. *John Adams*, *Cyane*, and *Constellation* were replaced by first-class-rated sloops-of-war. In each case, the new hull was as long as or longer than the hull of the frigate being replaced – a measure of warship growth in the 19th century. *Congress* was replaced by a 44-gun frigate, designed for a 24lb battery. Its replacement was the last sailing frigate built by the US Navy.

In only one case did the Navy build a frigate rated less than 44 guns after the War of 1812. When the *Macedonian* was replaced, it was by a 36-gun frigate. The hull, designed by Samuel Humphreys, had a different hull form from that of the original prize frigate – it was longer and larger. The upper works attempted to duplicate the appearance of the first *Macedonian*. The original figurehead was used, as were open railings appropriate to an earlier era. Launched in 1837, it spent only a short career as a frigate. It was cut down to a sloop-of-war in 1848.

OPERATIONAL HISTORY

The US Navy was born as a response to French privateers preying on American shipping. During the period when it used the frigates built for the Quasi-War with France, and incorporated the three prize frigates, the Navy fought three major wars and numerous actions against pirates and slavers. The Quasi-War with France ran from 1797 to 1801. The Barbary Wars ran from 1801 until 1807, then primarily against Tripoli, and flared up again in 1815. But undoubtedly the Navy met its biggest challenge during the War of 1812, which continued until March 1815.

The Quasi-War

The Quasi-War began as an attempt by France to intimidate the United States into reactivating its historic alliance with France, but it continued because the French discovered that preying upon American shipping was more profitable than going after British vessels. The United States retaliated by authorizing naval action against French privateers, national warships, and shipping.

At first the United States attempted to enforce its will with purchased warships – sloops-of-war. These proved inadequate to deal with large French warships, particularly the French frigates in the West Indies. Unfortunately it took a year between the time force was authorized against French ships in June 1797 and the time the first American frigate was ready to fight.

On June 26, 1798, the *Constellation* became the first frigate commissioned in the new US Navy. It was launched on September 9, 1797, in Baltimore harbor, but fitting the bare hull for sea took an additional ten months. The ship was intended to carry a battery of 26 18lb and ten 12lb smoothbore cannon. Instead it went to war carrying 24lb long guns instead of 18-pdrs. In 1797 the United States lacked a gun foundry industry capable of producing hundreds of cannon. To save time, it purchased cannon from Britain, then an ally. Eighteen-pound cannon were in high demand by the Royal Navy, but the British had surplus 24-gun cannon. The ships on which those were used – two-deckers and 64-gun ships-of-the-line – were being phased out.

B **ARMAMENT: 1800 AND 1812**

American frigates evolved in the dozen years between the launch of *Congress* and the period leading up to the War of 1812. As this plate illustrates, change was most apparent on the upper works – the quarterdeck and forecastle. The quarterdeck gun is shown, just forward of the mizzenmast in 1800 and 1812.

One big change was armament. In 1800, *Congress* carried 9lb long guns on its upper works. The long nine was 8½ft long, weighed almost 2,600lb, and was capable of throwing a 9lb iron ball 1,800 yards. By 1812, those guns had been replaced by 32lb carronades.

Carronades were much shorter than long guns. Mounted on slides rather than carriages, they required a smaller crew than a long gun. A 32lb carronade weighed only 2,000lb and could fire its 32lb ball 1,100 yards, but unless fitted with dispart sights, which allowed the gunner to sight parallel with the bore, it was unlikely to hit anything farther away than 100 yards. It also used a smaller charge of gunpowder than the long nine. The combination of the lighter barrel weight and smaller recoil meant carronades put less strain on a ship's timbers – although that was often offset by the American practice of cramming extra guns aboard when mounting carronades.

In 1800 *Congress* had open railings on the quarterdeck bulkheads. Gaps were filled by netting, and covered with weather cloths in foul weather to keep out spray. By 1812, the bulwarks were planked over for greater protection against enemy fire. This increased the weight of the upper works, exacerbating the tendency of American frigates – especially the smaller American frigates – to hog.

B ARMAMENT

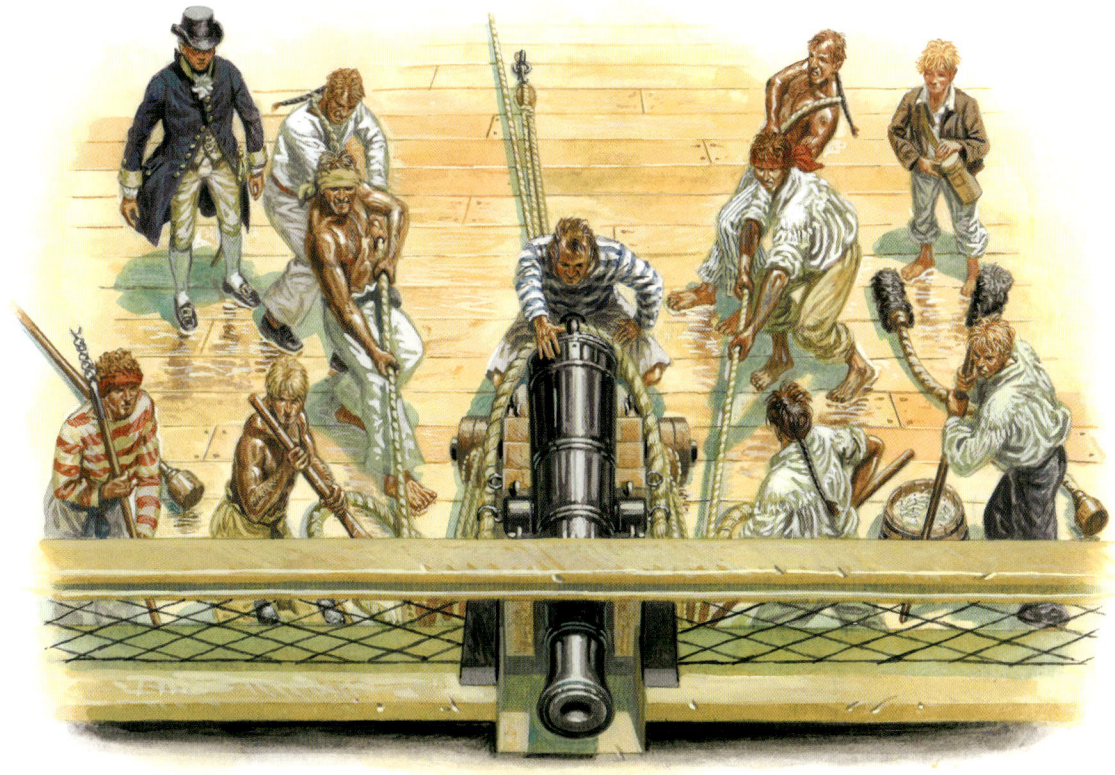

1800

1812

Constellation was the first frigate in active commission, and achieved an enviable record in the Quasi-War with France. This picture shows it later in its career, off Port Mahon, Menorca, in 1837. (USNHF)

When the *Constellation* was ready for sea, the United States had 24lb cannon available, but lacked 18-pdrs, and as a result the 24-pdrs were substituted for the designed battery. The firepower of its broadside was closer to that of a large two-decker than that of a standard 36-gun frigate. In turn, this firepower fitted with the philosophy of the new Navy.

American captains frequently overarmed their ships, cramming the largest guns possible into every gun port. Often, they would even cram one or two into the bridal ports, openings at the ships' bows intended to accommodate hawsers used to moor a ship. There was a price to be paid for overarming a ship. A 24lb long gun weighed 25 percent more than an 18-pdr, and used a 25 percent larger charge. The shock and recoil was significantly greater, and would shake apart ships designed for the lighter gun.

A separate problem was caused by the dead weight of the guns. Sailing frigates, narrower at the ends than amidships, had less buoyancy at the ends than in the middle – frigates had two rows of guns at the ends, and one in the middle, which meant that weight was concentrated at the ends of the ship. As a result, the hull would be pushed down at the ends, and pushed up in the middle, a condition known as hogging. Given time – a year or two was required – hogging would weaken a ship, often to the point where it was dangerous. The only cure was to rebuild the ship, replacing strained

Constellation in battle with the French 36-gun *Insurgente*. As was customary, *Insurgente* carried more guns than it was rated to carry. Truxton trumpeted that the French ship he captured carried more guns than his, but neglected to mention that *Constellation*'s broadside was 30 percent heavier than that of *Insurgente* due to the 24lb guns carried by the American vessel. (AC)

timbers. Alternatively a ship could be razeed – the quarterdeck and forecastle removed. This changed the frigate to a sloop-of-war, but also reduced the weight concentrations at the ends.

For the *Constellation*, that lay in the future. Commanded by pugnacious and capable Thomas Truxton, *Constellation* compiled an enviable record during the Quasi-War. On February 9, 1799, it encountered *Insurgente*, the French 36-gun frigate that was carrying 40 guns and a crew of 409 men. *Insurgente* had 12lb long guns on its gun deck, and 6-pdrs on the upper works. It also had four 36lb carronades, but the disparity of firepower between the two ships was simply too great. After a 90-minute fight, *Constellation* captured its foe. Truxton was a hero, *Constellation* was famous, and the US Navy had a new frigate – *Insurgent*, the anglicized version of the French name.

The victory led the US Navy to abandon building 24lb frigates for a dozen years. It gave Truxton the prestige he needed to push for the construction of smaller, supposedly handier frigates. Of course, the smaller ships needed to be built more lightly than Humphreys' big frigates. They were designed to carry only 18lb guns on the main deck, rather than the 24lb battery that gave *Constellation* its quick victory over *Insurgente*. The French had roughly handled the purchased American warships sent out in the war's first year. As the American frigates took to sea, larger than the purchased sloops-of-war, the tide turned – the US Navy swept the French national warships, privateers, and trading vessels from the Caribbean and West Indies.

The Navy's two heavy frigates, *Constitution* and *United States*, had lackluster records, more through bad luck and poor timing than through any naval shortcomings. Their large size and naval appearance encouraged French privateers to flee them. Except for *Constellation* and *Philadelphia*, the 18lb frigates, both 36- and 44-gun, had equally dismal results.

The lighter frigates met with more success. The four 32-gun frigates in the West Indies (*Essex* was sent to Batavia escorting a convoy), along with *Constellation* and *Philadelphia*, collected nearly a dozen privateers, a dozen French merchant ships, and recaptured over 20 American or British merchantmen between them. Additionally, *Boston* captured the French national warship *Berceau*, and *Constellation* fought and defeated the 40-gun *Vengeur*. The other eight frigates (including *Insurgent*) only bagged five privateers and recaptured three ships between them. The only loss among the Navy's frigates during the Quasi-War was the prize *Insurgent*. It disappeared at sea late in the war, and probably fell prey to a September hurricane.

The Quasi-War seemed to justify the focus on smaller frigates. But appearances were deceptive. When an American frigate captured a French warship, it always had an overwhelming superiority in broadside. Mounting 22 long 9-pdrs, and two 12lb long guns, for example, *Berceau* was overmatched by *Boston*'s 12lb main battery. Only the battle between *Constellation* and *Vengeur* showed a rough parity. *Vengeur*, rated at 40 guns, but carrying 52, had a long-gun broadside of 372lb. The *Constellation*, rearmed with 28 18lb guns, could fire a long-gun broadside of 252lb. Both ships carried carronades, with the *Constellation* carrying virtually a full gun deck of them to *Vengeur*'s four, but most of the battle was fought at ranges where they were not used.

The medal authorized by the United States Congress after *Constellation*'s victory over *l'Vengeur*. The front has a profile of Thomas Truxton, while the obverse depicts the battle. (USNHF)

WEIGHTS AND RANGES OF LONG GUNS AND CARRONADES

Cannon	Weight (pounds)	Range (yards) at 3 degrees elevation
Long Guns		
3 Pound	784	850
4 Pound	1,232	900
6 Pound	1,792	1,000
8 Pound	2,128	1,100
9 Pound	2,576	1,200
12 Pound	3,192	1,189
18 Pound	4,256	--
24 Pound	5,264	1,240
32 Pound	6,160	1,320
Carronades		
12 Pound	700	675
18 Pound	1,120	573
24 Pound	1,456	664
32 Pound	1,988	719
42 Pound	2,492	750

(Values from Howard Douglas, *A Treatise on Naval Gunnery*, 2nd edition)

In fact, the Navy did not need 13 active frigates. Three or four met the Navy's peacetime needs and only four to six were needed for a small war. The Navy built one yard where all of the laid-up frigates – those in ordinary – could be placed. It was built at the nation's new capital, the city of Washington, in the District of Columbia. The Washington Navy Yard was well up the Potomac River. The basin where the laid-up ships would be placed contained fresh water. Shipworm, the *teredo* mollusc that ate through hull planking, died in fresh water, and it was hoped the location would help preserve the hulls there.

Armament evolved during this period. Traditionally frigates had been armed with smooth-bore long guns. During the American Revolution the British invented a new ship's gun, the carronade. A short-barreled muzzle-loading gun, it could throw a ball four times heavier than a long gun with the same barrel weight. A carronade capable of firing a 24lb ball weighed 150lb less than a long gun firing a 6lb shot. Carronades had a shorter range than long guns, however. A 24lb carronade threw that ball half the distance of a 24lb long gun. On the other hand, it could fire three-quarters of the range of a 6lb long gun. At close range it was devastating – much more effective than a long gun of comparable barrel weight.

American frigate captains loved carronades. Carronades, shorter than long guns, could be placed in gangways along the waist, increasing the number of guns on the upper works. A frigate could more than double the weight of broadside with carronades, retaining a long-range punch with long guns on its gun deck. Captains began replacing light long guns on upper decks with carronades late in the Quasi-War, and added more and heavier carronades over the course of the decade.

The United States had previously negotiated peace with the three principal Barbary States on the North African coast – Algiers, Tunis, and Tripoli – in the 1790s. On May 10, 1801, Tripoli renewed its war against the United States. It fought the United States over the next four years, occasionally assisted by Morocco, another Barbary power. Tripoli had two large warships, the 26-gun *Meshuda*, and a 16-gun brig, as well as numerous smaller warships. All set out in search of American merchant shipping.

Philadelphia struck an uncharted reef off Tripoli on November 1, 1803, and was captured by Tripolean forces. The US Navy struggled for three months to retake or destroy their vessel. (AC)

The United States dispatched a squadron to the Mediterranean with two 44-gun frigates (*President* and *Philadelphia*), two smaller frigates (*Essex* and *Boston*), and two smaller warships. The vessels remained in the Mediterranean for a year, until relieved by ships from a second squadron sent from the United States. In turn, this would be relieved by a fresh squadron a year later. In some cases ships were retained in the Mediterranean an additional year before returning to America. Between 1801 and 1806 six squadrons were sent from the United States – every frigate except *General Greene* spent at least one cruise in the Mediterranean.

The ships sent in 1801 were in the best shape after the Quasi-War. Several frigates had already required major refits. *Constellation* required the most drastic rebuild – on top of the wear it suffered from carrying a battery of 24lb guns, it ran hard aground in April 1801. Only three years old, it was nearly rebuilt from the waterline up.

The need for regular repair and refitting continued through the Barbary Wars. Over-gunned frigates returned from a year or two of active cruising in the Mediterranean requiring a refit before again being used on active service. The most extreme examples, *New York* and *Boston*, returned from Barbary War cruises in such bad shape that they never were used again as warships – they ended their careers as receiving ships or stores hulks. *Constellation* also required a major reconstruction when it returned from the Mediterranean, receiving one in 1812, its second.

The standard and light frigates had undistinguished records during this war. The Navy was fighting gunboats and small, lateen-rigged privateers. These ran from frigates, except when circumstance gave them an advantage, and were better fought by armed schooners, brigs, and sloops-of-war. The only actions between American frigates and Barbary ships both involved *John Adams*. In 1803 it captured the Tripolean *Meshuda* (although flying a Moroccan flag it had been seized by that city) as it attempted to return to Tripoli with naval stores. Later that year it fought an inconclusive action with a 22-gun three-masted lateen-rigged warship.

Edward Preble, who commanded *Essex* on its Quasi-War cruise to Batavia, commanded the American Mediterranean Squadron when *Philadelphia* was captured, and led efforts to destroy it. (AC)

Frigates proved most useful blockading or assaulting ports, such as Tripoli and Derne. In these instances the 24lb frigates were better at bombardment than lighter frigates, and were more fortunate. During its first cruise *Philadelphia* ran aground on an uncharted reef off Tripoli on November 1, 1803, while chasing a Tripolean ship. Unable to free itself, it was beset by gunboats from Tripoli. Believing *Philadelphia* to be wrecked, its captain, William Bainbridge, surrendered. Tripolean forces soon refloated *Philadelphia*, and refitted their prize in Tripoli.

The rest of the American squadron, commanded by its energetic commodore Edwin Preble, concentrated its efforts on recovering or destroying *Philadelphia*. After several attempts to cut the frigate out of harbor or burn it, a party commanded by Stephen Decatur, then a lieutenant, succeeded in burning *Philadelphia* on February 16, 1804.

The United States and Tripoli negotiated a peace in 1805, but the United States kept squadrons in the Mediterranean for another two years. In 1807, HMS *Leopard* attacked the frigate *Chesapeake* off Hampton Roads as it began a voyage to the Mediterranean, an incident which is detailed later in the book, but which did lead directly to the withdrawal of the Mediterranean Squadron.

Philadelphia burning after a party of sailors led by Stephen Decatur boarded it on the evening of February 14, 1804. Nelson called the attack "the most bold and daring act of the age." (USNA-R)

The War of 1812

When the United States started its fight with Tripoli, Europe appeared to be headed for peace – France and Britain signed the Peace of Amiens in 1802 but this proved brief. Hostilities resumed in 1803 and a stalemate soon developed. France controlled Europe, but Britain controlled the waters off Europe, and economic war developed between the two countries. British sanctions fell most heavily on neutral nations, especially the United States. British fortunes were at their nadir in 1807 and they viewed America, "Brother Jonathan," as profiting at Britain's expense.

Resentments boiled over in June, 1807. *Chesapeake* was being sent to the Mediterranean to serve as Commodore James Barron's flagship in the American Mediterranean Squadron. Several members of *Chesapeake*'s crew had deserted from HMS *Leopard*, a British 50-gun two-decker. As Americans, they claimed to have been impressed into the Royal Navy against their will. The *Leopard*'s captain demanded their return, and was refused. On June 22 he intercepted *Chesapeake* off Hampton Roads, and again demanded the sailors. When the Americans refused, he ordered his gun crews to fire at the *Chesapeake*.

Chesapeake was unready for combat, for Barron had anticipated a long Atlantic crossing in which to get the ship on a war footing. The ship fired one gun, then surrendered. The British boarded, removed the four deserters, then left, refusing to accept *Chesapeake* as a prize. Barron and *Chesapeake*'s captain were cashiered for failing to have their ship ready for combat; US Navy ships thereafter sailed ready to fight as soon as they cleared port.

The incident poisoned Anglo-American relations. Jefferson responded with economic warfare of his own, supporting passage of the Embargo and Non-Intercourse Acts. But these devastated the American shipping industry instead, further exacerbating relations between Britain and the United States. America prepared to fight. Between 1807 and 1809, the three 24lb frigates were overhauled and commissioned. The Navy next turned its attention to the rest of its frigates. All of the 18lb and 12lb frigates needed refits or rebuilds by 1809. *New York*, *General Greene*, and *Boston* were in the worst shape,

Constellation not much better. *Essex* was rebuilt in 1809, *Congress* in 1810, *Chesapeake* in 1811, and *Constellation* in 1812.

The most problematic ships were the 12lb frigates. Small and vulnerable to larger frigates, the Navy recognized that they would be of limited use in any naval war with Britain. Only three were seaworthy: *Essex* had already been rebuilt, *John Adams* was in good shape, and *Adams* needed a refit.

Essex was rearmed almost exclusively with carronades – 40 32lb carronades and six 12lb long guns. A 32lb carronade was not an adequate replacement for its gun deck long 12s, but even armed as it had been in 1809 (28 12lb long guns, 18 32lb carronades), *Essex* would have been easy prey for a standard British frigate. The rearmament changed its function. Effectively it became a super-sized sloop-of-war, a commerce raider.

The Navy was similarly ambivalent about *Adams*. In 1812 *Adams* was cut in half, extended 12ft in length, and re-rated as a 36-gun frigate. After this was deemed unsatisfactory, the Navy removed the quarterdeck and forecastle, converting it to a 24-gun sloop-of-war.

When war was declared in June 1812, the US Navy had five frigates at sea – the three 24lb frigates plus *Congress* and *Essex*. *Chesapeake*, finishing its refit, would not sail until December 1812. *Constellation* had started its rebuild and *Adams* was being converted. *John Adams* still awaited recommissioning, and the remaining frigates were laid up at Washington Navy Yard.

Initially the American frigates operated in one big squadron under Commodore John Rodgers, the light and 24lb frigates operating in concert. While a successful strategy, it was soon superseded by frigates conducting individual cruises. This trend began when *Essex*, sailing to join this squadron, found and captured HMS *Alert*, a ten-gun sloop-of-war. Then *Constitution*, while detached from Rodgers' squadron, fell in with and destroyed HMS *Guerriere*, a 38-gun frigate. Soon afterwards, *United States* captured HMS *Macedonian*, which was made a prize and incorporated into the US Navy. From then on, the Navy was split into small groups or individual cruises. Groups disintegrated once at sea, as the captains pursued individual agendas. Individual cruising worked well through 1812, especially for the 24lb frigates and sloops-of-war, as they could find opponents that they could outclass and defeat. The standard and light frigates, *Essex* excepted, generally returned with negligible collections of merchant captures.

HMS *Leopard* firing into the unready *Chesapeake*. *Leopard* successfully recovered its deserted sailors, but at the cost of setting the United States and Britain on a collision course for war. (UNHF)

Commodore James Barron, one of the most senior officers in the US Navy, was suspended from the service for his role in the *Chesapeake* affair. (USNHF)

Essex sailed from the Delaware River in October 1812 with orders to rendezvous with *Constitution* in the South Atlantic. Failing to find *Constitution*, *Essex*, commanded by David Porter, sailed into the South Atlantic. Preying on British merchant shipping, it rounded Cape Horn into the Pacific, where it devastated the British whaling fleet, running wild until 1814.

In June 1813, however, American overconfidence turned to shock. *Chesapeake*, under a new commander, James Lawrence, was in Boston harbor, beginning a new cruise. Blockading the port was HMS *Shannon*, a 38-gun frigate, with a broadside almost identical to *Chesapeake*'s. Notwithstanding a new crew and a shortage of experienced officers, Lawrence sailed out to fight *Shannon*. Contemptuously disdaining an opportunity to rake *Shannon*, Lawrence fought a broadside-to-broadside action. *Shannon*'s superior crew soon made the difference. Within 15 minutes from the opening broadside, Lawrence was dying and *Chesapeake* taken.

Then *Essex* was finally run to earth. In January 1814 it was trapped in Valparaiso by two British frigates, *Phoebe* and *Cherub*. On March 28, 1814, Porter left port, during a storm. Losing a mast, he was then attacked by both British frigates while in neutral territorial waters. While he blamed the defeat on the carronade armament, he would have lost regardless, as he was fighting two ships while partially disabled.

By 1814, the big frigates still could muscle their way out to sea, and the sloops-of-war occasionally slipped out, but the smaller frigates found themselves trapped. *Constellation* finished its refit only to be caught in the Chesapeake estuary. It finished the war as a guard ship at Baltimore. *Macedonian* was blockaded in Connecticut, *Congress* in Portsmouth. *Adams* got to sea in January 1814, only to get trapped in the Penobscot River in August. It was burned on September 3, 1814, to prevent capture. The only frigate at sea other than the 24lb frigates was *John Adams*. It was being used as a cartel ship, carrying American diplomats to Europe and messages back. Its diplomatic duties placed it outside the war.

The British captured Washington, D.C., on August 24, 1814, but prior to British occupation the Navy burned the ships in the Washington Navy Yard. *New York*, *General Greene*, and *Boston* were all destroyed.

Essex captured HMS *Alert* when the British sloop mistook the American frigate for a merchantman, and attempted to capture it. The ten-gun British ship fell to the *Essex* with little resistance, and was the first British warship captured in the War of 1812. (FDRL)

By then, Navy policy had already changed. Only the 24lb frigates remained in commission. The remaining frigates were moored in port, their crews transferred to the inland lakes to man the fleets forming there. The Navy gained one more prize, in 1815: the post ship *Cyane*, captured in an unequal battle with *Constitution* on February 20, 1815. It entered the Navy's books as a 32-gun frigate on the strength of the guns it carried during the battle. At the end of the War of 1812 only five prewar frigates remained: *Constitution*, *United States*, *Constellation*, *Congress*, and *John Adams*. Four of these were Humphreys' designs – two of his three 24lb 44-gun frigates and the two 36-gun frigates.

HMS *Shannon* brings *Chesapeake* into Halifax harbor as a prize. The British crews are manning the rigging of both frigates, and crews in the harbor are cheering the arrival of the prize. (FDRL)

The war redefined the frigate for the United States. The experiences with *Chesapeake* and *Essex*, the impotence of the light and standard frigates, and the successes of the 24lb frigates, underscored the need to outgun America's foes. Virtually all future frigate construction reverted to Humphreys' vision – large ships capable of carrying heavy guns. Even the *Constellation* and *Congress*, de facto, were considered light frigates after the War of 1812. *John Adams* was the only light frigate left, the sole survivor of the subscription and contract frigates built during the Quasi-War. The US Navy added two prizes – *Macedonian* and *Cyane* – to its roster, both smaller than the new construction built during and after the War of 1812.

1815 and afterwards

While the US had been concentrating its efforts against the Royal Navy during the War of 1812, Algiers captured an American merchant ship. In addition, an American privateer sent British prizes it captured during that war into Tunis and Tripoli. Those rulers returned the prizes to the British. As a result the United States dispatched two squadrons to the Mediterranean, declaring war on Algiers on March 2, 1815. The first squadron, commanded by Stephen Decatur, sailed from New York harbor in May. It included the 44-gun *Guerriere*, the *Constellation*, the *Macedonian*, and seven smaller warships. The

Essex was finally run to earth by the Royal Navy in March 1814, off Valparaiso harbor, Chile. Attacked in neutral waters while trying to return to Valparaiso after losing a topmast, *Essex* was overwhelmed in an unequal fight with two British cruisers. (FDRL)

second, under William Bainbridge, sailed from Boston in July. It contained a ship-of-the-line, a 44-gun frigate, the *Congress*, and six smaller warships. Decatur arrived first. His squadron snapped up the Algerine frigate *Meshuda* almost immediately after arriving, before the *Meshuda* was aware that the squadron was in the Mediterranean. *Constellation*, still a fast sailer, led the chase, trapping the *Meshuda* so the rest of the squadron could catch up. Despite carrying 42 guns, *Meshuda* was probably the equivalent of a European frigate rated to carry 36 guns.

Decatur's squadron captured a 22-gun Algerine brig, then blockaded Algiers. The threat of losing the rest of his navy caused the Dey of Algiers to negotiate peace. Both sides returned captured ships and personnel. Algiers paid an indemnity and agreed to forgo further tribute. Decatur then sailed to Tunis and Tripoli where, under the guns of his squadron, he negotiated indemnities for American losses. By the time Bainbridge's squadron arrived, in August, the issue had been settled and Decatur's squadron sailed home.

Bainbridge's arrival was timely, however – the ruler of Algiers was considering restarting hostilities. Bainbridge showed the flag, revisiting the ports where Decatur had been. The presence of a second, even more powerful squadron convinced the Barbary States to remain at peace.

An on-again, off-again period of war and peace between Algiers and the United States continued until 1817, when a British and Dutch fleet destroyed the fortifications protecting the port. Nonetheless, the United States kept a squadron in the Mediterranean through the 1830s to keep watch on the Barbary States. Light frigates included in these squadrons included the *Constellation*, *Congress*, *John Adams*, and *Macedonian*.

The other major tasks facing the US Navy in the years following the War of 1812 were the suppression of piracy in the Caribbean and the suppression of slave ships off Africa. All of the surviving light frigates participated in those activities, although not necessarily as frigates. As the utility of the light frigates

David Porter in 1815, after returning from the Pacific. In addition to his Pacific cruise, Porter played an important role in suppressing Caribbean piracy during the 1820s. (AC)

D

USS *CHESAPEAKE* vs. HMS *SHANNON*

The battle between the *Chesapeake* and *Shannon* began when *Chesapeake* sailed out of Boston harbor at noon, June 1, 1813, to fight the blockading British ship. *Chesapeake* had a new captain, James Lawrence, and a crew assembled shortly before sailing. *Shannon*'s captain, Vere Broke, had been in command for years, and had an extensively drilled crew.

The battle opened at 1750hrs. Lawrence ignored an opportunity to sail behind *Shannon*, and fire his opening broadside into *Shannon*'s unprotected stern. Instead, he luffed up alongside *Shannon*, choosing a broadside-to-broadside gunnery duel. It was a gallant, but stupid decision. The superior training of the British crew soon told.

The plate depicts the moment when *Chesapeake*'s doom was sealed, at 1756hrs, six minutes into the battle. Lawrence had been carried below mortally wounded. Shot from *Shannon* had cut *Chesapeake*'s jibsail sheet and spanker brail. The jib, forward, flew free. The spanker, a big trapezoidal sail at the ship's stern, dropped down and filled. *Chesapeake*'s stern pivoted towards *Shannon*. Its port quarter gallery struck *Shannon* forward of its mainmast, and *Chesapeake* was locked to *Shannon* by the fluke of one of *Shannon*'s spare anchors.

Someone in *Shannon*'s tops dropped a grenade onto *Chesapeake*'s quarterdeck that landed in an arms locker and exploded, clearing the quarterdeck. Broke, seeing the opportunity, led a boarding party onto *Chesapeake*. Most of *Chesapeake*'s officers were already dead or wounded, and the only organized resistance to Broke's sally came from marksmen in the American's mizzentop. *Chesapeake*'s crew was forced below. After two unsuccessful attempts to regain the quarterdeck, the American crew surrendered. The fight took only 15 minutes, but *Chesapeake* had suffered 61 killed and 85 wounded out of its 379-man complement. *Shannon* lost 33 killed and 50 wounded out of 330 men.

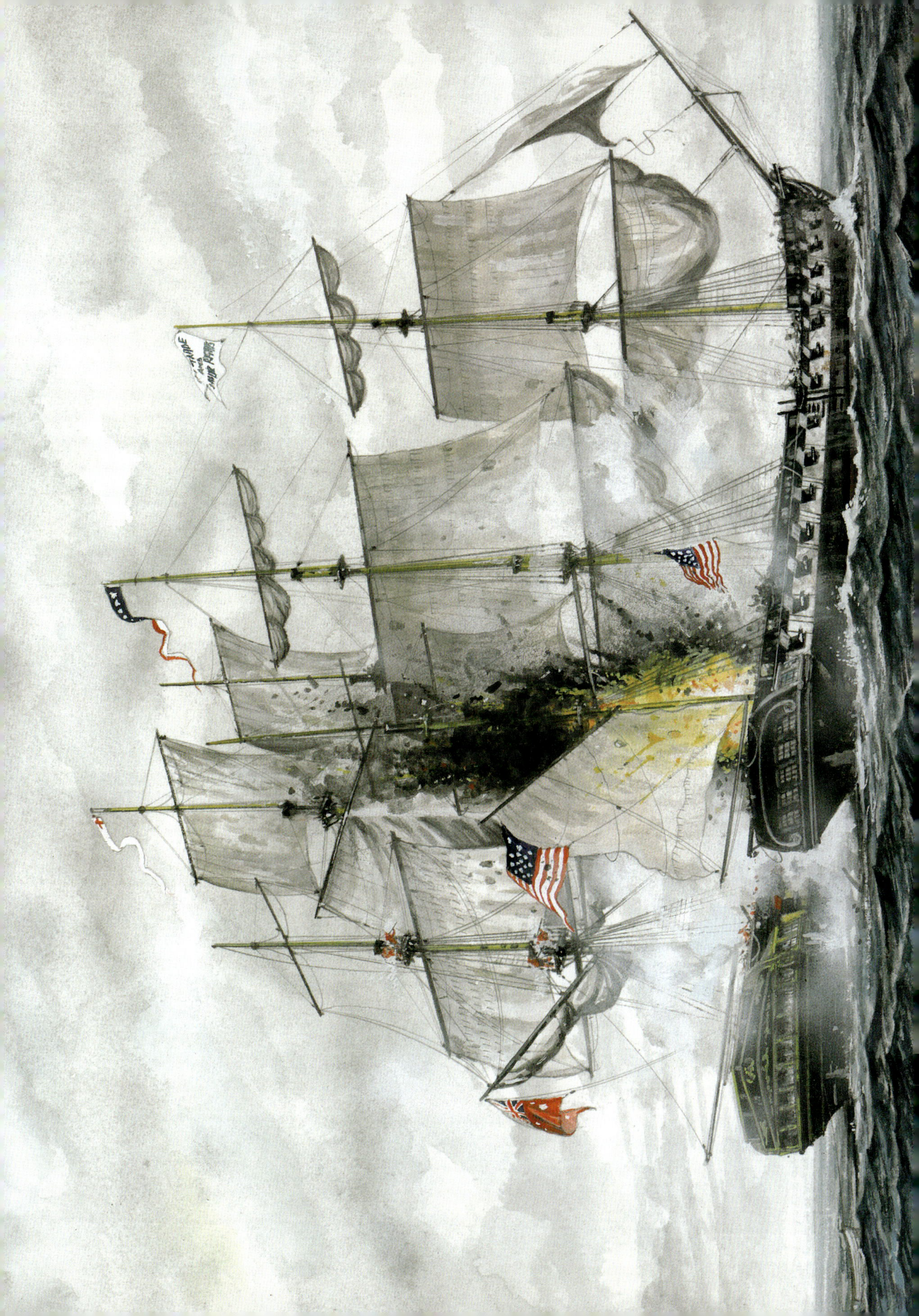

The second *Macedonian* leaving Hong Kong harbor in 1856. By this time the *Macedonian* had been cut down to a sloop-of-war, and it accompanied Perry's expedition to Japan. (FDRL)

lessened, and the ships aged, the surviving light frigates were either converted to sloops-of-war or scrapped. The first to be converted were the *John Adams* and the *Cyane*. Yet both ships were ultimately replaced with sloops-of-war, the *John Adams* in 1829, and *Cyane* in 1837.

Congress and *Macedonian* stayed as frigates for the remainder of their careers – both were eventually scrapped in the late 1820s, but were replaced by frigates. Because *Macedonian* was a prize, it was replaced with a ship of the same class. The second *Macedonian* was the only light frigate built by the US Navy after the War of 1812. Slightly larger than the first frigate, it retained much of the outward appearance of the original. It was unsuitable for carrying a 24lb battery, and was built for prestige rather than naval considerations. The second *Macedonian* was launched in 1836, and carried as a frigate for only a few years. In the late 1840s it too was cut down to a sloop-of-war. Eventually, it became a school ship, remaining in the Navy until 1877.

The final survivor was *Constellation*. It had an active career through the 1840s, but by 1845 the hull was worn out. Laid up from 1845 until 1853, it was finally scrapped in that year, to be replaced by a sloop-of-war of the same name. As with the *John Adams* and *Cyane*, the sloop replacing the frigate was larger than the original frigate. The United States' first commissioned frigate was replaced by its last sailing all-sail warship.

THE SHIPS

A line plan of the *Boston*. One of the few small frigates for which documented plans have survived, *Boston* typifies the appearance of the smaller 12lb frigates (US Navy)

Note on statistics: LBP is "Length Between Parallels" – typically the distance between the stem and sternpost. This is probably the best approximation of the waterline length. Breadth is maximum breadth or width of the ship. Depth of Hold measures the depth of the hold between the bottom of the ship and the berth deck. Draft is the loaded waterline. Displacement is given in long tons.

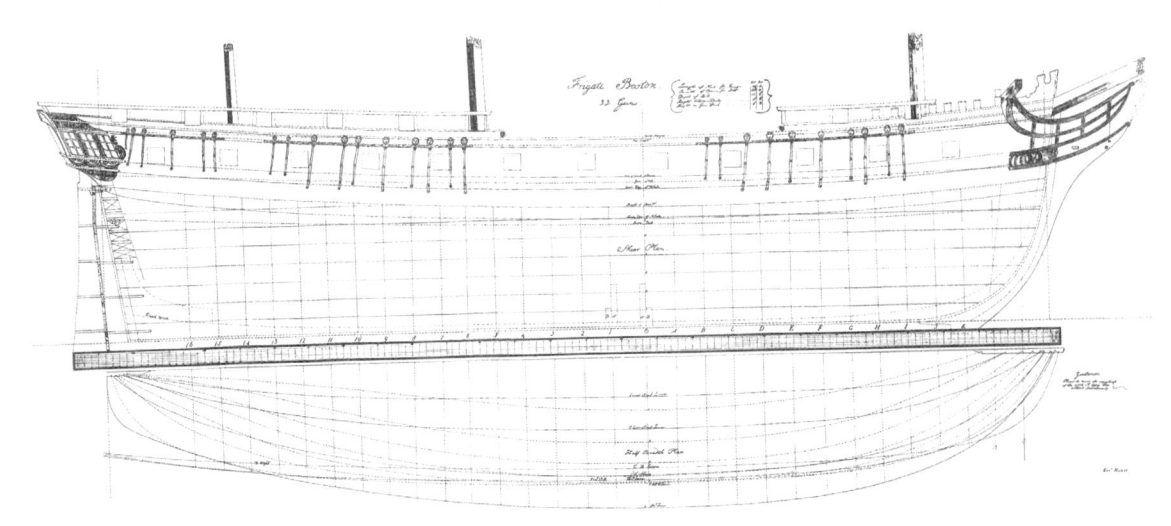

Dates are as accurate as possible. In some cases they are unknown and represent the author's best guess, indicated by a "?" Values are extracted from numerous sources, including *The Dictionary of American Naval Fighting Ships* (DANFS), Chapelle's *The History of the American Sailing Navy*, and Caney's *Sailing Warships of the US Navy*. DANFS is the primary source, unless the facts presented are superseded by more recent information.

Units are English – feet, inches, tons, and pounds – reflecting contemporary US Navy practice. Where information was unavailable the author calculated values from available information. The lack of uniformity in the shipbuilding industry – even within the US Navy – means that the values given are best-guess approximations.

Chesapeake under sail in light airs. The painting shows the frigate as it would have appeared shortly after the *Chesapeake* incident in 1807, when it patrolled the American coast. (USNHF)

The US Navy officially carried only three rates of frigate during the period 1794–1826: 44-gun, 36-gun, and 32-gun. The rating was independent of the size of the ship or the weight of its armament, but important in terms of crew size, pay, and money spent to support the ship. All 44-gun frigates were allowed crews that contained 292 seamen and boys, while a 36-gun frigate could carry 237 on its books. All of the 32-gun frigates from the 850-ton *Essex* to the 530-ton *Adams* were allowed 155 sailors and boys. In 1805, the *Chesapeake*, then rated as a 44, received the same budget as the other 44-gun frigates in the US Navy. It was re-rated as a 36-gun frigate in 1811 or 1812. The *Adams* was lengthened in 1812 and re-rated as a 36-gun frigate. Both *Chesapeake* and *Adams* were then entitled to the same crew as *Constellation*, *Congress*, and *New York*.

Because the rating reflected contemporary thinking about the ships, the frigates have been divided into these classes, with prize ships listed separately. While artificial, it is no more artificial than the often-used "original six," subscription frigates, and contract frigates.

Frigates rated 44 guns

Chesapeake

> **Laid down:** December 12, 1798, Gosport Navy Yard, Norfolk, VA
> **Launched:** December 2, 1799
> **First commissioned:** May 22, 1800
> **Dimensions – LBP:** 152ft 6in.; **Breadth:** 41ft; **Depth of hold:** 13ft 9in.; **Draft:** 22ft 4in.
> **Displacement:** 1,244 tons
> **Standard complement:** 340
> **Initial armament:** 28 x 18lb long guns, 16 x 9lb long guns

Chesapeake patrolled the southern coast of the United States and the West Indies during the Quasi-War, capturing French privateer *La Jeune Creole* on January 1, 1801. Laid up after the Quasi-War, it was recommissioned in April 1802, as flagship of the Mediterranean American squadron. It sailed from

Norfolk under Commodore Richard V. Morris, participating in the blockade of Tripoli. It returned on June 1, 1803, and was laid up at the Washington Navy Yard. In 1807 it was again sent to the Mediterranean as Commodore James Barron's flagship, but was forced to return to port, its Mediterranean voyage canceled after it was damaged in the *Leopard* incident. After a brief cruise off the American coast, *Chesapeake* was again laid up.

Re-rated as a 36-gun frigate, *Chesapeake* made two cruises in the War of 1812. On its first cruise – December 1812 through April 1813 – it captured five British merchant ships. It was subsequently seized, however, after a duel with HMS *Shannon* during its second voyage in May 1813. Purchased into the Royal Navy as a prize, it was too badly damaged to use. Sold out of the Royal Navy in 1820, it was broken up in Plymouth, England.

Philadelphia

Laid down: November 14, 1798, Humphreys, Hutton, and Delavue Shipyard, Philadelphia, PA
Launched: November 28, 1798
First commissioned: April 6, 1800
Dimensions – LBP: 157ft; **Breadth:** 39ft; **Depth of hold:** 13ft 6in.; **Draft:** 21ft 8in.
Displacement: 1,240 tons
Standard complement: 307
Initial armament: 28 x 18lb long guns, 6 x 12lb long guns, 6 x 32lb carronades

A detail of a painting showing Philadelphia entering the port of Tetuan, off the coast of Morocco, in 1803. It is jogging along under topsails. (USNHF)

Originally named *City of Philadelphia*, the *Philadelphia* was first commissioned in April 1800. It relieved *Constellation* at the Guadeloupe Station during the Quasi-War, and by war's end it had captured five French warships and recaptured six American merchant ships that had fallen into French hands.

After the Quasi-War, *Philadelphia* was dispatched in May 1801 to the Mediterranean as part of the first American squadron sent there to suppress the Barbary States. It returned to the United States in July 1802, having blockaded Tripoli and cruised the Straits of Gibraltar during its year in

E — USF PHILADELPHIA

Philadelphia was the second of two small "European-sized" 44-gun frigates designed by Josiah Fox. Smaller than the Humphreys 44s by nearly 20ft and the Humphreys 36-gun frigates by 5ft, it was longer than Fox's first 44-gun design, *Chesapeake*, by 5ft. Funds to build *Philadelphia* were raised though subscription by the town bearing its name. *Philadelphia* was rated as a 44-gun frigate throughout its career.

This plate shows *Philadelphia* as it appeared early in its career, during the Quasi-War. At the time, it had black sides with a wide buff stripe along the gunport strake, and buff-colored trim and scrollwork. The quarterdeck and forecastle bulwarks were open. Nettings or weather cloths filled the gaps.

At the time of its first cruise it was armed with 28 18lb cannon on its gun deck and 16 9lb long guns on its quarterdeck and forecastle. It carried 12 9lb guns on the quarterdeck and four on the forecastle. Later, during its Barbary War cruises, the long 9lb guns were replaced with carronades. *Philadelphia* carried 16 32lb carronades when it was sent to the Mediterranean in 1803. The spar, masting, and sail plan shown is typical of those used initially by US Navy frigates. Much smaller masts and spars were employed in the Quasi-War than during the War of 1812 and afterwards. (The picture on page 35 shows an 1817 sail plan of *Congress* by way of comparison.)

E

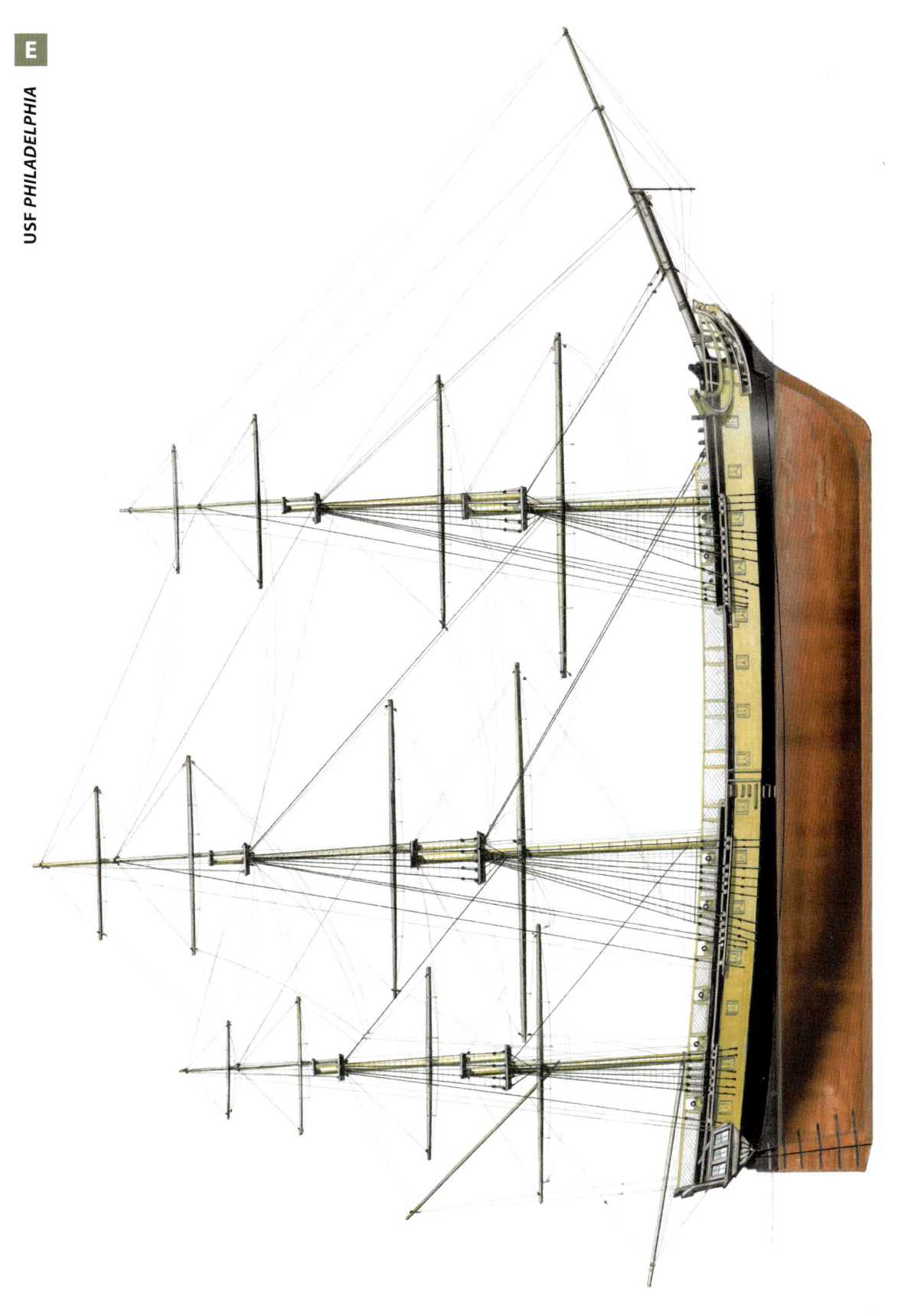

USF *PHILADELPHIA*

the Mediterranean. Laid up until May 1803, it was then recommissioned and sent to the Mediterranean, successfully recapturing the American brig *Cecilia* from Tripolitan forces and blockading Tripoli. On October 31, it ran aground on an uncharted reef in Tripoli harbor and, coming under fire, was forced to surrender. Over the next several months, the US Navy launched several unsuccessful attempts to recapture or destroy *Philadelphia*. On February 16, 1804, a party of volunteers led by Lieutenant Stephen Decatur succeeded in boarding and burning *Philadelphia*.

Frigates rated 36 guns

Constellation

Laid down: 1795, Stoddard Shipyard, Baltimore, MD
Launched: May 10, 1797
First commissioned: June 26, 1798
Dimensions – LBP: 163ft 3in.; **Breadth:** 40ft; **Depth of hold:** 13ft; **Draft:** 18ft 6in.
Displacement: 1,265 tons
Standard complement: 340
Initial armament: 28 x 24lb long guns, 10 x 12lb long guns (rated 36 guns)

Constellation first sailed to the West Indies during the Quasi-War in December 1798. During two years in the Caribbean and West Indies, it captured the 36-gun French frigate *Insurgente* and two large French privateers. It also decisively defeated the 40-gun frigate *Vengeur*, and recaptured three American merchant ships. Hull damage caused by the weight of its early Quasi-War battery (when it carried 24lb cannon), and grounding in Delaware Bay on April 1801, necessitated a refit in which *Constellation* was almost entirely reconstructed. *Constellation* served in the Mediterranean during the Barbary Wars, from May 1802 until November 1805, taking an active part in the fight against Tripoli and Tunis, then was laid up at Washington Navy Yard until 1812.

At the start of the War of 1812, *Constellation* underwent a major refit. By the time the refit was completed in January 1813, the vessel was blockaded in the Chesapeake. It concluded the war as a floating battery off Baltimore. Thereafter, *Constellation* joined the final actions against the Barbary States in 1815–17, participating in the capture of the Algerine frigate *Meshuda* on June 17, 1815, as part of Stephen Decatur's squadron.

From 1819 through 1845, *Constellation* alternated between active duty and refits. It participated in the eradication of pirates in the West Indies, the Seminole War, and the Opium War. Circumnavigating the globe in the 1840s, *Constellation* served on virtually every station of the US Navy. In 1845 it was laid up at Norfolk Navy Yard, where it was broken up in 1853.

Sloop-of-war *Constellation* as a training ship in 1910. Although this ship was frequently confused with the Federal-era frigate of the same name during much of the 20th century, it is not the same ship. Designed and built as a sloop-of-war during the 1850s, it was the last sailing warship of the US Navy. (LOC)

34

Congress

Laid down: 1795, Hacket Shipyard, Portsmouth, NH
Launched: August 15, 1799
First commissioned: December, 1799
Dimensions – LBP: 163ft 3in.; **Breadth:** 40ft; **Depth of hold:** 13ft; **Draft:** 18ft 6in.
Displacement: 1,265 tons
Standard complement: 340
Initial armament: 24 x 18lb long guns, 12 x 12lb long guns

Sent with *Essex* to escort a merchant fleet to the Dutch East Indies in January 1800, *Congress* was forced to return to port six days after sailing from New York having lost a mast. Following repairs at Hampton Roads, *Congress* served in the West Indies for the rest of the Quasi-War, recapturing one American merchant brig. Laid up in 1801 at Washington Navy Yard, the vessel was sent to the Mediterranean Squadron in 1804. It cruised in the Mediterranean for 11 months before returning to the Navy Yard.

After an extensive rebuild in 1811, *Congress* was recommissioned. It captured 14 prizes in three cruises during the War of 1812. In January 1814, while at Portsmouth, New Hampshire, *Congress* was stripped of its crew, which was sent to the lakes fleets, and was idle for the rest of the war.

Congress participated in the final squadrons sent to suppress the Barbary States after the War of 1812, in 1815–16. From October 1822 through April 1823, it was involved in anti-piracy patrols in the West Indies, and then was used to transport US ministers to Spain and Argentina. After 1824, it was laid up in Washington Navy Yard. In 1829 it was towed to Norfolk as a receiving ship and was broken up in 1834, after being found unfit for repair.

Sail plan of *Congress* drawn in 1816 by Charles Ware. Note the oversized gaffs on all three masts, and the skysails over the royals. (USNHF)

New York

Laid down: August, 1798, Peck and Carpenter, New York City, NY
Launched: April 24, 1800
First commissioned: October 1800
Dimensions – LBP: 144ft; **Breadth:** 37ft; **Depth of hold:** 11ft 9in.; **Draft:** 20ft 4in.
Displacement: 1,130 tons
Standard complement: 340
Initial armament: 26 x 18lb long guns, 10 x 9lb long guns

The *New York* was the first frigate designed by Samuel Humphreys. One of five "subscription" frigates, it was the last frigate launched and commissioned in the United States during the Quasi-War.

The *New York* saw service in only two short cruises. It served briefly in the Quasi-War, escorting a convoy from New York to the Caribbean from October to December 1800. It patrolled briefly around Guadeloupe from December 1800 until March 1801, when word of the peace arrived in the West Indies. Returning to the Washington Navy Yard, it was laid up until August 14, 1802. It was then sent to the Mediterranean to reinforce the squadron sent to fight the Barbary States – *New York* served with the Mediterranean Squadron until November 1803, helping to blockade Tripoli. It arrived at Washington Navy Yard in December, and laid up in reserve there. It remained in Washington until it was burned on August 24, 1814, to prevent its capture by the British.

A line plan of the frigate *New York*, as it would have appeared late in its career. This possibly was drafted after 1809, when the Navy was considering the practicality of rebuilding *New York*. (US Navy)

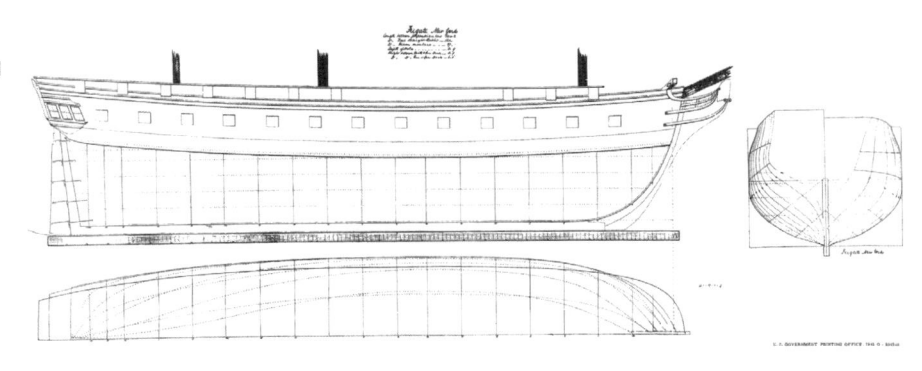

Macedonian (II)

> **Laid down:** February 28, 1833, Norfolk Navy Yard, Portsmouth, VA
> **Launched:** November 1, 1836
> **First commissioned:** October 1837
> **Dimensions – LBP:** 164ft; **Breadth:** 41ft; **Depth of hold:** 18ft; **Draft:** 21ft 6in.
> **Displacement:** 1,341 tons
> **Standard complement:** 489
> **Initial armament:** Unknown – probably 18lb long guns on the main deck and 8-in. shell guns on the spar deck

Built to replace namesake prize frigate *Macedonian*, this ship was the only small frigate built by the US Navy after 1801. Built to a new, modern hull design, the Navy attempted to duplicate the outward appearance of the prize in its successor.

Macedonian served on anti-piracy duty in the West Indies, and slave-trade suppression between 1839 and 1847. In 1847 it was disarmed, and sent under civilian control to carry famine relief supplies to Ireland. In 1852 *Macedonian* was converted to a sloop-of-war by removing its upper works, and as a sloop-of-war it served in Perry's expedition to Japan (1852–54) and on patrol in the North Pacific for three years after that.

Macedonian served from 1857 through 1861 in the Home Squadron and the Mediterranean, and as a warship in the Civil War from 1861 through 1863, mainly in the West Indies. In 1863 it was assigned as a school ship at the United States Naval Academy, serving in that role through 1871. Laid up at Norfolk until 1875, it was sold into merchant service, where it remained until the hull burned in 1913.

Frigates rated 32 guns

Essex

> **Laid down:** April 13, 1799, Enos Briggs, Salem, MA
> **Launched:** September 30, 1799
> **First commissioned:** December 17, 1799
> **Dimensions – LBP:** 140ft; **Breadth:** 37ft; **Depth of hold:** 12ft 3in.; **Draft:** 19ft 10in.
> **Displacement:** 850 tons
> **Standard complement:** 300
> **Initial armament:** 26 x 12lb long guns, 10 x 6lb long guns

Essex spent the Quasi-War escorting an American merchant convoy to the Dutch East Indies. Commanded by Edward Preble, *Essex* sailed from New York on January 6, 1800, for Batavia, returning November 1800.

A model of *Essex* showing its appearance at the time of its launch. The model, built by Charles Cozewith, shows a ship with more delicate upper works than it had during the War of 1812. (AC)

It then sailed for the Mediterranean in May 1801, commanded by William Bainbridge, part of a squadron sent to fight Tripoli. It returned from the Mediterranean in 1802, undergoing an extensive refit in Washington Navy Yard. It again sailed for the Mediterranean in August 1804, remaining until peace was signed with Tripoli in 1806.

Laid up at Washington Navy Yard until February 1809, *Essex* then patrolled American waters. At the start of the War of 1812, it was the only light frigate on active duty. Commanded by Captain David Porter, on its first cruise from June through September 1812 it captured 11 merchant prizes and the 10-gun Royal Navy sloop-of-war *Alert*.

Sailing next to the South Atlantic, in January 1813 it rounded Cape Horn into the South Pacific. *Essex* preyed upon the British whaling industry in the Pacific, capturing 11 prizes. In January 1814 it was trapped in neutral Valparaiso harbor, now in Chile, by British frigates *Phoebe* and *Cherub*. Following a long blockade it was eventually attacked and captured on March 28, 1814.

Boston

Laid down: August 28, 1798, Edmund Hartt Yard, Boston, MA
Launched: May 24, 1799
First commissioned: July 1799
Dimensions – LBP: 134ft; **Breadth:** 34ft 6in.; **Depth of hold:** 11ft 6in.; **Draft:** 18ft 6in.
Displacement: 700 tons
Standard complement: 220
Initial armament: 24 x 12lb long guns, 8 x 9lb long guns

Essex (center, with topmasts struck) surrounded by whaling prizes in Nukahiva in the Marquesas Islands in late 1813. Porter refitted *Essex* in this remote location. (AC)

Boston, drying sails in harbor, while in the Mediterranean during its 1801–02 cruise there. (AC)

Boston's subscription frigate during the Quasi-War, *Boston* sailed from its namesake city to the West Indies on July 24, 1799, commanded by Captain George Little. In 1799 it captured three French ships, and recaptured an American merchant schooner. In 1800, *Boston* also took two French privateers, three merchant vessels, and fought and defeated a flotilla of nine armed barges, sinking five before the rest fled. More successes followed. On October 12, 1800, *Boston* encountered the French national warship *Berceau*, a large 24-gun corvette equal to a small frigate in size and firepower. In a furious action, Boston captured the French vessel. *Berceau* was later returned to France under the terms of the peace treaty settling the Quasi-War in March 1801.

Boston was extensively refitted in the summer of 1801, and sent to Europe as part of America's Mediterranean Squadron in the war against Tripoli. *Boston* remained in the Mediterranean for a year, participating in the blockade of Tripoli and escorting American merchant shipping.

After returning from the Mediterranean in October, 1802, *Boston* was laid up at Washington Navy Yard. It remained there until August 1814, when it was burned to prevent its capture by the British.

John Adams

Laid down: 1798[?], Paul Prichard, Charleston, SC
Launched: June 5, 1799
First commissioned: August 8, 1799
Dimensions – LBP: 139ft; **Breadth:** 32ft; **Depth of hold:** 16ft 4in.; **Draft:** 19ft 8in.
Displacement: 544 tons
Standard complement: 220
Initial armament: 24 x 12lb long guns, 2 x 9lb long guns, 6 x 24lb carronades (rated 28 guns)

Built as Charleston's subscription frigate, *John Adams* patrolled around Cayenne, French Guiana, and in the West Indies around Guadeloupe during the Quasi-War. During its cruise from October 1799 through January 1801, it took two French merchant vessels and a privateer, and recaptured six American merchantmen.

Laid up in mid-January 1801, the frigate was recommissioned and sent in October 1802 to the Mediterranean to reinforce the American squadron fighting Tripoli. In May 1803, *John Adams* captured a 20-gun Tripolean cruiser, *Meshuda*. In June, assisted by the schooner *Enterprise*, *John Adams* captured a second 22-gun Tripolean warship. Involved in numerous actions against Tripolean gunboats during 1803, it served as squadron storeship in 1804–05.

Laid up from 1805 onward, *John Adams* was undergoing a refit in Boston when the War of 1812 started. Moved to New York to complete the refit, a combination of the British blockade and a lack of sailors kept it in port thereafter. In early 1814, however, it served as a cartel ship, sailing under a flag of truce. It concluded the War of 1812 on that duty, carrying the American delegation to Europe, and dispatches between Europe and the United States.

Between 1815 and 1819 the frigate was active in anti-piracy duties in numerous places, including the Mediterranean, West Indies, Florida, and South America. Reduced to a 24-gun sloop-of-war in 1820, it was again on anti-piracy duty in the West Indies from 1823 through 1829. It was scrapped in 1829.

Adams

Laid down: July 30, 1798, Jackson & Sheffield, Brooklyn, NY
Launched: August 6, 1799
First commissioned: September 1799
Dimensions – LBP: 113ft; **Breadth:** 34ft; **Depth of hold:** 10ft 9in.; **Draft:** 17ft 4in.
Displacement: 530 tons
Standard complement: 480
Initial armament: 24 x 12lb long guns, 6 x 24lb carronades

John Adams after being cut down to a sloop-of-war. In this picture it is shown chasing Caribbean pirates in 1822. (USNHF)

The smallest frigate built for the US Navy, *Adams* was constructed under Navy contract. *Adams* made two cruises in the Quasi-War, recapturing a dozen American or British ships from French prize crews, and capturing two French privateers and five French merchant vessels. During the Barbary Wars, the *Adams* made one cruise, sailing to the Mediterranean in June 1802 with Commodore Richard Morris' squadron and participating in activities against Tripoli. Returning in November 1803, it was laid up until 1805.

From 1805 to 1806 *Adams* patrolled the Atlantic coast of the United States. In 1809, it was commissioned to enforce the Embargo Act; after 1809, it was laid up at Washington Navy Yard, serving as a receiving ship. In June 1812, it was completely rebuilt. Cut in half amidships, it was extended 15ft and re-rated as a 36-gun frigate. The rebuild proved unsatisfactory, so *Adams* was razeed to a 24-gun sloop-of-war.

Blockaded in the Chesapeake, *Adams* finally escaped to sea in January 1814. On its first cruise it captured five British merchantmen. Its second cruise, in May, took it from the Newfoundland Banks to Ireland, during which it took five more merchant prizes. It was trapped in the Penobscot River on its return, and was burned in September 1814 to prevent its capture by the British.

General Greene

Laid down: August 1798, Talman & DeWolf, Warren, RI
Launched: January 21, 1799
First commissioned: June 1799
Dimensions – LBP: 124ft 3in.; **Breadth:** 34ft 8in.; **Depth of hold:** 17ft 3in.; **Draft:** 20ft 3in.
Displacement: 655 tons
Standard complement: 480
Initial armament: 24 x 12lb long guns, 6 x 6lb long guns

Designed by Benjamin Talman (who also designed *Warren*), *General Greene* was a "small" 32-gun frigate built under Navy contract in 1799. It never carried more than 30 guns. It began its first cruise during the Quasi-War, sailing to Havana in June 1799. It subsequently suffered storm damage, and then lost 20 men to yellow fever during repairs in Havana.

Refitted in Newport, it sailed with *Boston* to San Domingo in December 1799. Spending six months off Santo Domingo, it supported Toussaint L'Ouverture against rebel forces. While there it captured a schooner, freed an American schooner, and captured the French privateer *Hope*. It returned to Providence in July 1800, remaining idle for the rest of the Quasi-War. After May 1801, it was sent to the Washington Navy Yard, where it was laid up for the rest of its career. It was burned on August 24, 1814, with the Washington Navy Yard.

Insurgente was the first major warship added to the US Navy by capture. It is shown here being pursued by *Constellation*, prior to the battle leading to its capture. It served as an American frigate until lost at sea in a storm. (AC)

Prize Frigates

Insurgent

Laid down: November 1791, Lorient, France
Launched: April 27, 1793
Captured and first commissioned (USN): February 9, 1799
Dimensions – LBP: 175ft; **Breadth:** 45ft; **Depth of hold:** 14ft 4in.; **Draft:** unknown
Displacement: 1,726 tons
Standard complement: 480
Initial armament: 26 x 12lb long guns, 10 x 6lb long guns, 4 x 36lb carronades (rated 36 guns)

After its capture by *Constellation*, *Insurgente* was placed under command of Truxton's first lieutenant, John Rodgers, and refitted as an American warship in the West Indies. It spent the next two months sailing in company with *Constellation*. Ordered back to the United States, it was formally purchased for $84,000 and renamed *Insurgent*. Placed under the command of Captain Alexander Murray, *Insurgent* sailed for European waters in August 1799. It returned from this cruise in March 1800, having captured one French ship, and recaptured four American merchantmen taken as prizes.

Departing Baltimore in July 1800 with a new captain, Patrick Fletcher, the frigate touched briefly at Hampton Roads. On August 8 it departed with orders to patrol the waters between the United States and the West Indies. Never seen again, *Insurgent* was presumed lost in a hurricane that hit the West Indies on September 20, 1800.

Macedonian (I)

Laid down: May 1809, Woolwich Dockyard, Britain
Launched: June 2, 1810
Captured: October 25, 1812

First commissioned (USN): April 1813
Dimensions – LBP: 156ft; **Breadth:** 38ft 9in.; **Depth of hold:** 13ft 6in.; **Draft:** 19ft 4in.
Displacement: 1,325 tons
Standard complement: 306
Initial armament: 28 x 18lb long guns, 2 x 12lb long guns, 2 x 9lb long guns, 16 x 32lb carronades (rated 38 guns)

Captured by Stephen Decatur off the Canary Islands, *Macedonian* reached New London, Connecticut, where it was purchased into the US Navy. Refitted and readied for sea, *Macedonian* was blockaded in port for the rest of the Quasi-War. In 1814, its crew was sent to reinforce the lakes squadrons. After the end of the War of 1812, *Macedonian* participated in the final actions against the Barbary States, and as part of Stephen Decatur's squadron, it took part in the capture of the Algerine frigate *Meshuda*, on June 17, 1815. It remained in the Mediterranean until 1818.

From January 1819 to March 1821, *Macedonian* was assigned to the Pacific coast of South America, assisting American ships during colonial revolts in South America. From 1823 through 1826 it served in anti-piracy efforts in the West Indies, then from June 1826 through October 1828 it was on the Pacific Station. *Macedonian* returned to Hampton Roads in October 1828, was decommissioned, and broken up later that year at Norfolk.

Cyane

Laid down: 1796 Frimsbuy[?], Britain[?]
Launched: March 25, 1847
Captured: February 20, 1815
First commissioned (USN): 1819
Dimensions – LBP: 120ft 4in.; **Breadth:** 31ft 6in.; **Depth of hold:** 8ft 6in.; **Draft:** 13ft 6in.
Displacement: 420 tons
Standard complement: 480
Initial armament: 22 x 32lb carronades, 8 x 18lb carronades, 2 x 12lb long guns (rated 32 guns)

The Royal Navy rated *Cyane* a 24-gun post ship – a post captain's command, but not a frigate. The ship mounted guns on its quarterdeck and forecastle, and was carrying 32 guns when USS *Constitution* captured it on February 20, 1815. For prestige reasons it was purchased into the US Navy as a 32-gun frigate.

The War of 1812 ended shortly after it arrived in the United States, and it spent the next four years laid up. Recommissioned in 1819, it spent 1819–20 off West Africa, and 1820–21 in the West Indies, suppressing the slave trade and piracy. Following that, it was laid up, then cut down to a 20-gun sloop-of-war. Recommissioned in 1824, it spent 1824–25 in the Mediterranean, and 1825–27 on the Brazil Station. Laid up in Philadelphia Navy Yard afterwards, it sank at its mooring in 1835. Raised the following year, it was then broken up.

Macedonian in 1820 while on anti-piracy duty in the Caribbean. This was a task better suited to the small frigates and sloops-of-war rather than the heavy frigates. (AC)

Cyane (right) joined the US Navy involuntarily, being captured by *Constitution* (center) during a night engagement off Madeira, on February 20, 1815. It remained in the US Navy for 20 years. (FDRL)

GLOSSARY

Berth deck: The deck below the gun deck on an American frigate, where the crew slept.

Carronade: A short-barreled smoothbore gun that could throw a much heavier ball than a traditional long gun whose barrel weighed the same. A 12lb carronade weighed less than a 4lb long gun, but fired a ball that weighed three times as much. It threw its shot, however, a shorter range than a long gun of the same caliber.

MARINES IN THE FIGHTING TOP

Between the top of the lower mast and the bottom of the upper mast, sailing ships had a platform called a top or mast top. It was not the "crow's nest" beloved of boys' fiction and pirate stories, although among its uses was a perch for lookouts. It was also used to hold the shrouds that guy the topmasts, as well as a platform from which to work on the sails carried by the lower masts, the courses. The platform was an excellent place to station sharpshooters and grenadiers in battle. Hence, on a frigate (or other warship) the top is often called the fighting top.

To provide sharpshooters, as well as for use in boarding parties and maintaining shipboard discipline, each frigate had a contingent of Marines aboard – seagoing soldiers who belonged to the United States Marine Corps. The size of the contingent was based on the rating of a frigate. The 44-gun frigates (including *Chesapeake* and *Philadelphia*) were authorized 60 Marines, of which 50 were privates. Thirty-six gun frigates carried 47 Marines, with 40 privates. Thirty-two gun ships (including the "small" 32s, such as *General Greene*) had 35 Marines, with 30 privates.

The plate shows a contingent of Marines on a 32-gun frigate's maintop during battle. The period would be between 1801 and 1805, during the Barbary Wars. At that time, Marine uniform consisted of a blue jacket with red facings, a red vest, white breeches and gaiters, and white cross-belts. The uniforms also came with a round hat, edged in yellow. Often, in battle the jackets and vests would be removed for greater freedom of movement. As would prove typical for the Marine Corps, their uniforms started as Army surplus – when the Marine Corps was founded it was issued leftover uniforms from "Mad Anthony" Wayne's Legion. The immediate precursor to the United States Army, the legion had used a non-European organization, but was disbanded when the Army reorganized on traditional regimental lines.

James Lawrence was courageous but foolish. An easy victory over the British sloop-of-war *Peacock* while commanding the *Hornet* led him to underestimate the fighting quality of the Royal Navy. He paid for his impetuosity with his life. (AC)

Forecastle: A raised platform at the front of the ship generally used to manage the anchors and foremast and to provide protection from a head sea.

Frigate: A sailing warship with one full gun deck and additional guns mounted on the forecastle and quarterdeck. A warship with a full gun deck and additional guns only mounted on the quarterdeck is sometimes called a jackass frigate.

Gun deck: Deck on an American frigate or sloop-of-war carrying the main battery of guns. Considered the upper deck of the ship, despite the spar deck above it. A ship-of-the-line or two-decker will have more than one gun deck. These are identified by their position – upper, lower, or middle (if there are three gun decks).

Hogging: The condition when the weight at the ends of a ship exceeds the buoyancy provided by the ends, especially when buoyancy amidships exceeds its weight. The ends of the ship sag down, and the middle is pushed up, giving the appearance of a razorback hog. This strains the ship's timbers, weakening them.

Lateen sail: A triangular sail with the top edge hung from a long yard which mounted at its middle to the top of the mast. The lateen yard is rigged fore-and-aft, allowing a ship to sail close to the direction of the wind.

Lateen-rigged: A ship carrying one or more lateen masts.

Quarterdeck: A partial deck above the main or gun deck where the navigation and operation of the ship is managed. Generally the quarterdeck starts between the main mast and the mizzen mast.

Rake: To fire a broadside down the length of the opposing warship, either from the stern or bow. Raking shot caused much more damage because it went the length rather than the breadth of a ship.

Razee: A ship that has had its upper deck removed, converting it into the next smaller class of warship. A ship-of-the-line is razeed to a frigate. A frigate is razeed to a sloop-of-war.

Ship-of-the-line: A ship-rigged (q.v.) warship with at least two full gun decks and additional guns on the quarterdeck and forecastle that is strong enough to stand in the line of battle. Ships-of-the-line mounted 64 to 140 guns.

Ship rigged: A ship with at least three masts, all carrying square sails, is said to be ship rigged.

Sloop-of-war: A warship with guns mounted only on the gun deck. Three-masted sloops-of-war are often called ship-sloops, and two-masted sloops-of-war are often called brig-sloops. Occasionally a sloop-of-war has additional guns mounted on the quarterdeck. These are also referred to as "post" ships or jackass frigates.

Spar deck: A flush deck on an American frigate consisting of the forecastle, quarterdeck, and the gangways connecting the quarterdeck and forecastle. Generally there is an opening amidships spanned by skids on which the spare spars and ships boats are kept.

Squaresail: Four-sided sails, occasionally square but more often trapezoidal, set on spars, and perpendicular to the length of the ship. American frigates generally mounted five, and sometimes six, sails on their masts. From lowest to highest were the course, topsail, topgallant, royal, skysail, and moonsail or hope-in-heaven. (The name of the sixth sail varied widely.)

Two-decker: A ship-rigged warship with two full gun decks and additional guns on the quarterdeck and forecastle that is too weak to stand in the line-of battle. These 44-gun to 56-gun warships are miniature ships-of-the-line useful for convoy duty and as flagships. They are often confused with frigates because they mount a similar number of guns.

Weather cloth: A piece of canvas placed over gaps in railings, which reduces the spray and water hitting the deck in high seas.

BIBLIOGRAPHY

Allen, Garner W., *Our Naval War with France*, Houghton Mifflin, New York (1909)
_____, *Our Navy and the Barbary Corsairs*, Houghton Mifflin, New York (1905)
Caney, Donald L., *Sailing Warships of the US Navy*, US Naval Institute Press, Annapolis, MD (2001)
Chapelle, Howard I., *The History of the American Sailing Navy*, W. W. Norton, New York (1949)
_____, *The History of American Sailing Ships*, W. W. Norton, New York (1935)
De Kay, James T., *Chronicles of the Frigate Macedonian, 1809–1922*, W. W. Norton & Company, New York (1995)
Douglas, Howard, *A Treatise on Naval Gunnery*, 2nd ed., John Murray, London (1829)
Dudley, William S. (ed.), *The Naval War of 1812, A Documentary History*, 3 vols, Naval Historical Center, Department of the Navy, Washington, D.C. (1965)
Gardiner, Robert, *The Heavy Frigate – Eighteen-Pounder Frigates, Vol I, 1778–1800*, Conway Maritime Press, London (1994)
_____, *The Naval War of 1812*, Chatham Publishers, London (1998)
Harland, John, *Seamanship in the Age of Sail*, US Naval Institute Press, Annapolis, MD (1990)
James, William, *The Naval History of Great Britain, from the Declaration of War by France in 1793, to the Accession of George IV*, Richard Bentley, London (1859)
Knox, Dudley (ed.), *Naval Documents Relating to the United States Wars with the Barbary Powers*, 6 vols, US Government Printing Office, Washington, D.C. (1939–44)
_____ (ed.), *Naval Documents Relating to the Quasi-War between the United States and France*, 7 vols, US Government Printing Office, Washington, D.C. (1935–38)
_____ (ed.), *Register Of Officer Personnel, US Navy and Marine Corps and Ship's Data 1801–1807*, US Government Printing Office, Washington, D.C. (1945)
Lavery, Brian, *The Arming and Fitting of English Ships of War, 1660–1815* (Conway's History of Sail), Conway Maritime Press Ltd (1999)
Mooney, James L. (ed.), *The Dictionary of American Naval Fighting Ships*, US Government Printing Office, Washington, D.C. (1977)
Moore, Sir Alan, *Sailing Ships of War, 1800–1860*, Halton and Truscott Smith Ltd, London (1926)
Peterson, C. J., *History of the United States Navy*, Jas. B. Smith and Co., Philadelphia (1857)
Porter, David, *Journal of a Cruise Made to the Pacific Ocean by Captain David Porter, in the United States Frigate Essex, in the Years 1812, 1813, and 1814*, 2 vols, Bradford and Inskeep, New York (1815)
Robotti, Frances D. and Vescovi, James, *The USS Essex: and the Birth of the American Navy*, Adams Media Corporation, Holbrook, MA (1999)
Roosevelt, Theodore, *The Naval War of 1812*, G. P. Putnam's Sons, New York and London (1900)
Takajian, Portia, *32-Gun Frigate Essex (Anatomy of the Ship)*, Phoenix Publications, Cedarburg, WI (1990)
Tucker, Spencer, *Arming the Fleet, U.S. Navy Ordinance in the Muzzle-Loading Era*, United States Naval Institute Press, Annapolis, MD (1989)
Wegner, Dana, *Fouled Anchors: The* Constellation *Question Answered*, David Taylor Research Center, Bethesda, MD (1991)

INDEX

Figures in **bold** refer to illustrations.

Adams, USS 14, 15, 25, 26, 31, 39
Alert, HMS 25, **26**
Algiers 6, 27
 see also Barbary States and War
Alliance, USS 8, 9, 15
America, USS 8

Bainbridge, Capt William 23, 28, 37
Barbary States and War 6, 12, 20–23, 27–28
Barron, Cdre James 24, **26**, 32
Berceau **5**, 19, 38
Bon Homme Richard, USS 7
Boston, USS **5**, 14, 19, **30**, 37–38, **38**
 and Barbary Wars 23
 sail plan of 12, **13**
 and War of 1812: 24, 26
Bourbon, USS 8

cannon
 see also carronades
 configurations of 6–8, 8–10, 11, 12, 14, 15, 16, **17**, 18, 19, 25, 31, 40–41
 French Navy 9–10
 Royal Navy 7, 12
 weights and ranges 22
carronades 22, 25, 26
Cecilia 34
Cherub, HMS 26, 37
Chesapeake, USS 4, **12**, 14, 28, **29**, 31, **31**, 31–32, 44
 and Barbary Wars 23
 and War of 1812: 24, 25, **25**, 26, **26**, 27
Chesapeake-Leopard Affair 14, 24–25, 28, **29**
Congress, USS 10, 11, 15, 16, 28, 30, 31, 35, **35**
 and War of 1812: 25, 26, 27
Constellation, USS 10, 11, 12, 15, 16, **18**, 19, **19**, 28, 30, 31, 32, 34, **34**, 42
 and Barbary Wars 20, **21**, 23
 and War of 1812: 25, 26, 27
Constitution, USS 11, 19, 25, 26, 27, 43, **44**
Continental frigates 8–10
crews 31
Cyane, HMS and USS 15, 27, 30, 43, **44**

Decatur, Lt Stephen 23, 24, 27, 28, 34, 43
designs 6, 6–15, 7, **10**
 for US Federal Navy 10–11
Dey of Algiers 28

Essex, USS 14, 15, 19, 31, 36–37, **37**, 40–41
 and Barbary Wars 23
 and War of 1812: 25, 26, **26**, 27, **27**

Falkland, HMS 8
Fox, Josiah 11, **11**, 12, 14
French Navy 8, 9–10, 11–12, 16–19
frigates
 of 32 gun rating 36–42
 of 36 gun rating 34–36
 of 44 gun rating 31–34
 characteristics of 30–31
 conversion
  from ships of the line 10
  to sloops 15, 19
 designs 6, 6–15, 7, **10**
 for US Federal Navy 10–11
 funded by US cities 11, 35
 hull weakness (hogging) 18–19
 operations 16–30
 prizes 42–43
 and US shipbuilding experience 8

General Greene, USS 14, 23, 24, 26, 39, 42, 44
glossary 44, 46–47
Guerriere, HMS and USS 25, 27
guns see cannon

Hackett, James 9
Hackett, William 9, 15
Halifax harbor **27**
Hancock, USS (later HMS Isis) **8**, 8, 11
hogging (hull weakness) 18–19
Humphreys, Joshua 8, 10–11, 14, 27
Humphreys, Samuel 15, 35

Incorruptable 9
Indefatigable, HMS 12
Insurgent(e) (French and USS) 12, 15, **18**, 19, 34, **42**, 42–43
Isis, HMS (earlier USS Hancock) **8**, 8, 11

Jefferson, Thomas, 3rd President of the US 24
John Adams, USS 14, 15, **20**, 23, 28, 30, 38–39, **39**
 and War of 1812: 25, 26, 27

La Jeune Creole 31
Lawrence, Capt James 26, **46**
Length Between Parallels (LBP) 30

Leopard, HMS 23, 24, **25**, 32
 see also Chesapeake-Leopard Affair
Little, Capt George 38

Macedonian (I), HMS and USS 15, **15**, 25, 26, 27, 28, 30, **30**, 42–43, **43**
Macedonian (II), USS 15, 36
marines 44, **45**
Meshuda (Algiers) 22, 23, 28, 34, 43
Morris, Cdre Richard V. 32, 39

Nelson, Adm Horatio 24
New York, USS 15, 23, 24, 26, 31, 35, **36**

Philadelphia, USS 14, **14**, 15, 19, **22**, 23, **24**, **32**, 32–34, **33**, 44
Phoebe, HMS 26, 37
piracy 6, 16, 28
Pomone, HMS (formerly French) 8, 10
Porter, Capt David 26, **28**, 37
Preble, Cdre Edward 23, **23**, 36
President, USS 11, 23

Quasi-War 11, 12, 14, 15, 16–19

Randolph, USS 8, 9, 10
Retaliation, USS 11
Rodgers, Cdre John 25
Royal Navy 9, 12
 and Barbary States 6
 and War of 1812 24–27

Serapis, USS 7
Shannon, HMS 4, 26, **27**, 28, **29**, 32
ships of the line 6, 7
shipworm 22
slave ships 28
Spanish Navy 10
A System of Masting (Truxton) 12

Truxton, Cdre Thomas **10**, 11–12, 18, 19, **19**, 20
Tunis 6
 see also Barbary States and War

United States, USS 11, 19, 25, 26
US shipbuilding experience 8

Vengeur 19, **19**, 20, **21**, 34

War of 1812: 15, 24–30
Warren, USS 8, 9
Washington, USS 11
Washington D.C. 26
Washington Navy Yard 22, 26